Who Was
Che Guevara?

by Ellen Labrecque

illustrated by Jerry Hoare

Penguin Workshop

For Jeff—EL

PENGUIN WORKSHOP
An Imprint of Penguin Random House LLC, New York

Text copyright © 2019 by Ellen Labrecque. Illustrations copyright © 2019 by Penguin Random House LLC. All rights reserved. Published by Penguin Workshop, an imprint of Penguin Random House LLC, New York. PENGUIN and PENGUIN WORKSHOP are trademarks of Penguin Books Ltd. WHO HQ & Design is a registered trademark of Penguin Random House LLC. Printed in the USA.

Visit us online at www.penguinrandomhouse.com.

Library of Congress Cataloging-in-Publication Data is available upon request.

ISBN 9780399544019 (paperback)   10 9 8 7 6 5 4 3 2 1
ISBN 9780399544033 (library binding)   10 9 8 7 6 5 4 3 2 1

Contents

Who Was Che Guevara?

In December 1951, Ernesto Guevara, who later became known simply as "Che," and his friend Alberto Granado set off on a motorcycle adventure from Córdoba, Argentina. They planned to ride all the way to the top of South America. Twenty-three-year-old Che was studying to become a doctor, but he was taking a break from medical school. He wanted to explore the world.

On their journey, Che and Alberto met a husband and wife high in the Andes Mountains of Chile. The couple was dirty and very thin. The day was cold, but they wore only flimsy clothes and didn't even have a blanket to share between them. They were heading to work in a sulfur mine. Digging for sulfur is dangerous—the sulfur burns workers' lungs and eyes. It is like working with poison all day long. The couple would labor twelve to fifteen hours a day and not get paid much money. It was the only work they could find. They needed to feed and take care of their children, who they had left back home with a neighbor.

Che and Alberto shared their tea, cheese, bread, and blankets with the couple. Che was heartbroken. He didn't think it was fair for these people to work hard in such terrible conditions and still be nearly starving.

The next morning, everybody went their

separate ways, but Che never forgot the husband and wife he had met in the mountains of Chile. He realized he wanted to help the poor people who were sometimes taken advantage of by wealthy business owners.

Che Guevara didn't live a very long life. After his nine-month motorcycle trip with Alberto, he became a revolutionary leader who fought for the poor. He tried to make big changes—like overthrowing leaders of countries—in order to bring about his ideas of justice and equality. He was willing to die for his beliefs—and kill for them, as well. Because of this, some people think Che is a villain. Others think he is a hero. But almost everyone understands the impact he made on the world.

CHAPTER 1
A Brave Boy

Ernesto Guevara was born on June 14, 1928, in the port city of Rosario, Argentina, in the lower half of South America. His parents, Ernesto Guevara Lynch and Celia de la Serna, owned a five-hundred-acre plantation. They grew a type of evergreen tree—called yerba mate (say: YER-bah mah-tay)—that is used to make strong tea.

The plantation was on the banks of a river in a rain forest, where yerba mate grows best. Ernesto was the oldest child in the Guevara family. But the family grew, and he eventually had two brothers and two sisters.

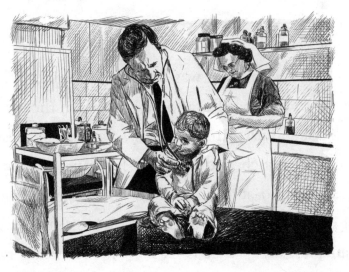

When Ernesto was two years old, his mother took him swimming in the local river. Soon after their swim, Ernesto started coughing and couldn't stop. He also began to have trouble breathing. His parents took him to the doctor. The doctor said Ernesto had asthma—a lung disease that makes it difficult to breathe and causes coughing and wheezing.

Ernesto was often sick. He had coughing fits and periods when it was hard to breathe. His parents took him to see many doctors to try to help him. One doctor told them the air in the rain forest was too damp and humid for Ernesto's little lungs. The doctor suggested that they move to a place with drier air, where it would be easier for Ernesto to breathe. In 1932, the family moved to Alta Gracia, a resort town near a mountain range.

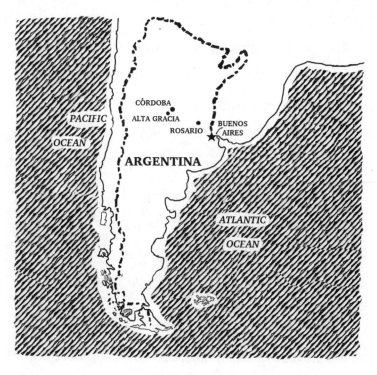

The crisp mountain air helped Ernesto, but it didn't cure him. He still suffered asthma attacks. As a result, Ernesto barely went to school until he was nine years old. Instead, his mother taught him at home. While he was sick, he spent long hours reading in bed. He loved the adventure stories written by Jules Verne.

Ernesto's mom and dad let their children run free. When Ernesto was healthy enough to play outside, he climbed tall trees, ran on railroad tracks, and explored abandoned mine tunnels with his brothers and sisters. He wanted to prove he wasn't sick or weak. He wanted to be brave.

Jules Verne (1828–1905)

Jules Verne was a French science-fiction writer. Science fiction is a type of story that explores ideas like imaginary worlds, time travel, and life on other planets. Some of Verne's most famous books are *Twenty Thousand Leagues Under the Sea*, *Journey to the Center of the Earth*, and *Around the World in Eighty Days*. Many of his most popular stories were later turned into movies.

Ernesto's family was friendly with everyone in Alta Gracia—wealthy families and poorer ones, too. Ernesto played with children of maids and cleaning ladies as easily as he played with the richest kids in town. His mother and father showed Ernesto how to be generous. They always made sure they had enough food at home for any guest to share a meal with them.

Because of his family's openness to bending the rules, Ernesto's house usually had plenty

of children running around. The kids were all allowed to ride bikes through the front door, around the living room, and then outside into the backyard.

In 1942, Ernesto began high school. Because Alta Gracia didn't have one, fourteen-year-old Ernesto took a bus to a school in Córdoba, over twenty miles away. He rode the bus back and forth for one year until his family decided to move there.

CHAPTER 2
Finding His Way

Ernesto was growing into a bold young man. A classmate in Córdoba described him as "incredibly sure of himself and totally independent in his opinions." He didn't care what people thought, and this made people like him even more.

Ernesto was handsome, with smooth skin and broad shoulders, but he was a sloppy dresser who bragged about not washing his clothes. He would

say to his friends, "It's been twenty-five weeks since I washed this shirt." Ernesto was sometimes called "Chancho," which means "the pig" in Spanish. He was actually proud of this nickname.

Ernesto still had asthma attacks. When he had to stay inside to recover, he spent days reading anything he could get his hands on. He also began writing and taking notes on all the books he was reading.

When Ernesto was healthy, he played on a rugby team—a sport that's like a mix of soccer and American football. Although he wasn't a big kid, Ernesto was fast and fearless. He wasn't afraid to tackle somebody hard or be tackled.

The coach of Ernesto's team was Alberto Granado, a student at the University of Córdoba. Despite Alberto being six years older than Ernesto, the two became good friends. They both loved to read and could talk about books for hours.

During this time in Ernesto's life, the world was changing. World War II was raging in Europe. Argentina stayed out of the war, but its people still supported different sides. Some Argentinians were for the Axis side (Germany, Italy, and Japan), while others supported the Allies (Great Britain, France, the Soviet Union, and the United States). Changes in leadership were also happening constantly in Argentina. Juan Perón, who would rule for the next eleven years, became the leader of Argentina in 1946.

Juan Perón

Ernesto stayed out of politics. He was looking for adventure, not to take sides on political issues.

Ernesto graduated from high school in 1946, about the same time he turned eighteen. He planned on studying engineering in college. But his plans changed when his grandmother became sick and died. She was ninety-six years old and had lived a long and happy life, but Ernesto was still crushed. He wished there were some way he could have helped her. Soon after his grandmother's death, Ernesto decided to become a doctor. Still struggling with his own asthma, he also hoped to try to find a cure for his condition, too.

"I dreamed of becoming a famous researcher," he said.

Ernesto applied and was accepted to medical school at the University of Buenos Aires, in the capital of Argentina.

CHAPTER 3
The Adventure Begins

Ernesto studied hard in medical school, but whenever he had the chance, he traveled. At the end of his third year, in January 1950, he attached a small motor onto his bicycle and rode from the coast into the middle of Argentina. He was on

the road for six weeks and traveled nearly 2,500 miles. One stop Ernesto made on his adventure was to see his old rugby coach, Alberto Granado.

Alberto was now doing medical research at a leper colony in the town of San Francisco del Chañar. Ernesto, who was doing his own medical research on allergies, loved talking to his friend about their studies.

Leprosy

Leprosy is a disease that has scared people since ancient times. It affects the skin and the nerves, and it can cause large bumps and sores to form all over the body. People with leprosy can lose their fingers, toes, and even their noses. Some people were so afraid of catching this disease, the sick were sent away to "leper colonies" to live apart from the rest of the community. Today most cases of leprosy can be cured with medicine.

While traveling all over Argentina, Ernesto began to write in his journal every day. This is something he would keep up for the rest of his life. At the end of his six weeks, Ernesto went back to medical school for his fourth and final year. But a great desire to explore the world had taken hold of him.

Ernesto was soon presented with another opportunity for adventure. His good friend Alberto wanted to take a trip on his motorcycle, nicknamed La Poderosa II (The Mighty II), from Argentina north all the way to Venezuela. He

La Poderosa II

asked if Ernesto wanted to join him. Ernesto, now twenty-three, still had two semesters left of medical school, but he wanted to go. He promised his mother that he would eventually go back and finish his medical degree. In December 1951, the two friends set off on a journey that would change Ernesto's life forever.

CHAPTER 4
The Motorcycle Diaries

Ernesto and Alberto didn't want to stay in fancy hotels on their trip. They wanted to meet people of all different backgrounds and see how they lived—especially the poor.

The Motorcycle Diaries Map

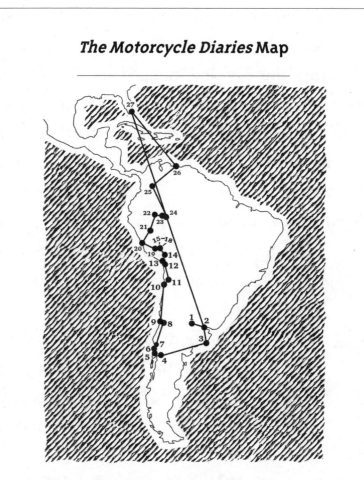

This is the path of Ernesto's trip, which lasted from December 1951 to August 1952. Ernesto wrote a book about his journey called *The Motorcycle Diaries*, which was published in 1993.

The young men didn't have a lot of money, so this plan worked perfectly. They rode La Poderosa II during the day and camped on the side of the road at night. Ernesto still had asthma, so sometimes they had to rest for several days before they hit the road again.

La Poderosa II was an old motorcycle. It broke down a lot and had to be fixed. The young men  did odd jobs, like washing dishes or taking out trash, in return for free repairs, food, or a place to sleep for the night. When they had to, they also begged. Ernesto took photos and kept a daily journal of their adventures.

A couple of months into the trip, while visiting a coastal city in Chile, their motorcycle broke down for good. Ernesto and Alberto continued their journey on foot, hitching rides on the backs of trucks, or sneaking onto ships. Even though Ernesto wasn't a doctor yet, he had been taught how to help people who were sick or injured. People treated them generously, giving them food or a place to stay. In return, Ernesto would treat sick people who couldn't afford to see a "real" doctor.

While in a city in Chile, a restaurant owner asked Ernesto to check on one of the elderly waitresses. The woman had asthma, just like Ernesto, but she also had a weak heart. She lived in a dirty one-room house and couldn't afford any medication.

"The poor thing was in a pitiful state," Ernesto wrote. Ernesto gave her some of his own asthma medicine and tried to make her as comfortable as possible. But he was amazed by how unfair it all was. Ernesto could not understand why someone who worked so hard could not afford even a little medicine to help make herself well.

Soon after treating the sick woman, Ernesto and Alberto hitched a ride on the back of a truck in the Andes Mountains. Along the way, they met a very poor man and woman.

"The couple, numb with cold, were huddling against each other," Ernesto wrote. They were hungry, tired, and had no money. They were

going to work in a sulfur mine.

Working at the mine was the couple's only chance of supporting their family. The company that owned the mine made millions of dollars by selling sulfur, which can be used to make things like detergents, gunpowder, and other explosives.

This poor couple barely made enough money to live, while the owners of the large company—who lived in the United States—got rich from all the hard work the couple did. The miners in Chile were uneducated. The sulfur mine was their only chance at work. Ernesto would never forget this meeting.

CHAPTER 5
The Journey Continues

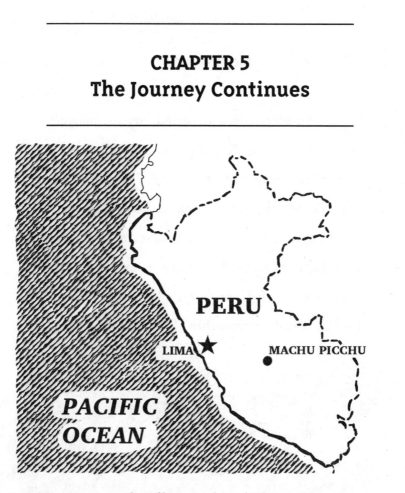

Ernesto and Alberto headed to Peru next, where they visited Machu Picchu. Ernesto told Alberto, "I have dreamed of visiting the ruins of Machu Picchu since I was a boy."

Machu Picchu

Machu Picchu is a deserted city in the Andes Mountains. It was built by the Inca people in the fifteenth century. The city is built of stone and filled with plazas, temples, houses, and walkways. There are thousands of stone steps and terraces that were used for farming. Although it is over five hundred years old, the city is still partially intact because of the skill and craftsmanship of the Inca builders.

Plants and trees covered Machu Picchu for centuries, and only a few people knew that this ancient city existed. In 1911, a local farmer named Melchor Arteaga led American explorer Hiram Bingham to the site. Bingham told the world about the site in his book *Lost City of the Incas*. Today Machu Picchu is one of the major tourist attractions in South America.

After leaving the ruins of Machu Picchu, Ernesto and Alberto visited a leper colony. The two men weren't afraid of the patients. They stayed for days, playing sports and games with everyone there. When they were ready to leave, the patients with leprosy gave Ernesto and Alberto a raft they had built themselves. The two men were very grateful. They boarded their raft and headed down the Amazon River.

They eventually made it to Colombia and then on to Venezuela, where Alberto decided to remain and work at another leper colony. Ernesto had to get back home to finish medical school. He contacted a relative who helped arrange for racehorses to be flown back and forth between the United States, Venezuela, and Argentina. He told Ernesto he could grab a ride on one of his planes, but first he had to go to Miami, Florida.

Ernesto accepted the offer. He spent his time in Miami reading in the library and going to the beach. He made friends with a man who owned a restaurant there and who was nice enough to give him free meals.

Ernesto, now twenty-four, finally returned to Argentina in August 1952. He had been gone for nine months and had traveled over five thousand miles. He still planned to finish school. But he now saw the world in a different way.

"I am not the person I once was," Ernesto wrote. "All this wandering around 'Our America with a capital A' has changed me more than I thought." After spending his whole life in Argentina, he had now seen much of the entire continent of South America. His journey had been a completely different sort of education, one that didn't rely on books and classrooms to teach the lessons of how difficult life was for so many people.

"I began to come into close contact with

poverty, with hunger, with disease," he explained
later. "And I began to see that there was something
that seemed to me almost as important as being
a famous researcher or making some substantial
contribution to medical science, and this was
helping those people."

CHAPTER 6
A Doctor at Last

Ernesto returned to medical school right away. He studied day and night to pass his exams. In March 1953, just seven months after his return, Ernesto became a doctor. And just four months later, he set off on another adventure. This time with his friend, Carlos "Calica" Ferrer, and now on a train instead of a motorcycle. They headed

north through Bolivia, Peru, and Ecuador. Over the next five months, they traveled all the way through South and Central America to arrive in Guatemala in January 1954.

At this time, the president of Guatemala was Jacobo Árbenz, and he was working to help the poor people of his country. One of his ideas was land reform. President Árbenz was taking land owned by rich people and big corporations, then redistributing it to the poor. Ernesto was so glad to see someone in charge thinking this

Jacobo Árbenz

way. He decided to stay in Guatemala and support the president.

While in Guatemala, Ernesto met Hilda Gadea. Hilda was from Peru, and she was a

communist. She became Ernesto's girlfriend. And Ernesto began learning about communism.

Ernesto and Hilda spent a lot of time together talking about communist ideas. They both agreed that a communist system

Hilda Gadea

might work better for poor people. A communist government would attempt to share the wealth of its country with all of its people, instead of just

with the rich. Hilda also introduced Ernesto to her friends, who were communist revolutionaries. These were people who wanted to change the country and were willing to use violence to bring about that change.

In the 1950s, the United States had a lot of businesses in Guatemala. One was the United Fruit Company, which was the biggest landowner in the whole country. That meant that one American company owned more of Guatemala than the Guatemalans did! The United Fruit Company grew bananas in Guatemala, then exported and sold them all over the world. The company made a lot of money. And  while they gave lots of it to Guatemalan leaders and their rich friends, they paid very little to the workers on their farms.

Communism

Communism is a type of government in which individuals do not own land, homes, or businesses. The government controls these things, along with all factories and farms. Many communist governments do not allow freedom of speech or freedom of the press.

Karl Marx

A German man named Karl Marx is considered to be the "father of communism." Marx said that governments would have to be overthrown—a revolution would have to take place—in order for communism to completely take root in a country. This was an idea that inspired some people to begin their own revolutions.

A nickname was given to countries in Central America, like Guatemala, that grew so much fruit for foreign businesses. They were called "banana republics." Ernesto disliked this system very much. He didn't want other countries, like the United States, owning Guatemala's land and paying Guatemalans hardly anything, while making millions of dollars for themselves.

Whenever he saw an American on the streets in Guatemala, Ernesto would say, "Too many gringos! Too many gringos!" *Gringo* is a term for any person, but especially an American, who is not from a Spanish-speaking country.

When President Árbenz began taking land away from the United Fruit Company to give to the poor people of Guatemala, the United States government got involved to protect American businesses. It trained and paid soldiers at military bases outside the country to invade Guatemala. Under attack, Árbenz had to flee the country.

The United States then put in his place another man, who let the United Fruit Company keep its land.

Ernesto was extremely angry. He and other revolutionaries soon planned to overthrow this new leader—to remove him from power—using guns and violence. Their secret operation never had a chance. The new Guatemalan government learned about their plan and started to arrest anybody who was involved with it. Ernesto, Hilda, and some of their other friends fled to Mexico to avoid going to jail. In this moment, Ernesto felt even more strongly about what he wanted to do with his life: He wanted to be a revolutionary.

Ernesto was now convinced "of the necessity for armed struggle," explained Hilda. She meant that Ernesto's refusal to accept Guatemala's new government officials led him to believe that violence was an acceptable solution to the problem.

CHAPTER 7
Mexico

For the first time since Ernesto had graduated from medical school, he began working as a doctor. He was working at a local hospital in Mexico City when a patient from Cuba came in. Ernesto became friendly with the patient and soon began hanging out with him and his group of Cuban friends. They called Ernesto "Che"— which is a common Argentine expression for "friend." It is like calling somebody "buddy" or "pal." The nickname stuck with him for the rest of his life.

One night, Che's new friends invited him to dinner. There, he met a man named Fidel Castro. Fidel told Che that a small group of wealthy people controlled the country of Cuba, while the peasants did all the work. The peasants were the poor farmers who worked so hard for so little. Che knew that many South and Central American countries were run like this, too. In Che's travels, he had seen the same thing again and again. Poor people were working hard to increase the wealth of rich people but barely making enough money to live.

Fidel told Che that he and his brother, Raúl, were plotting to overthrow the Cuban government. Fidel asked Che whether he wanted to join their army as a medical doctor. Che said yes. He was ready to stop traveling for fun and start helping people fight for their rights. Although he wasn't Cuban, Che understood their cause.

"A person like Che did not require elaborate arguments," Fidel said later. "It was sufficient for him to know that those people were inspired by genuinely revolutionary and patriotic ideals. That was more than enough."

Fidel Castro (1926–2016)

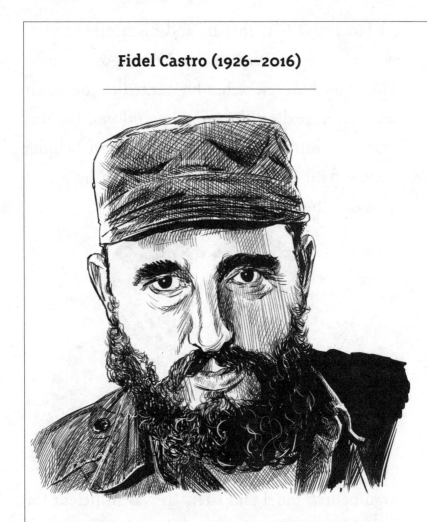

Fidel Castro was born in Cuba and grew up on a sugarcane farm. He became a lawyer and defended the poor people of his country.

In the 1950s, Fidel started a revolution in Cuba against its dictator, Fulgencio Batista. Fidel and his army battled Batista and his troops for two years. On January 1, 1959, Batista fled the country, and Fidel took over as its new ruler. Fidel did some things to help poor people, like give them free health care and education. But he also didn't allow the Cuban people to have their own opinions. He forced out all foreign businesses, especially the ones owned by US companies. He led Cuba from 1959 to 2006 as a communist dictator. Fidel passed on his power to his brother, Raúl Castro, in July 2006. Fidel died ten years later at age ninety.

Soon after Che agreed to join Fidel's army, Hilda and Che were married. In February 1956, their daughter Hildita was born. Che, now twenty-seven, had a wife and a daughter, but he was still determined to help Fidel and the people of Cuba. He would have to leave Hilda and Hildita behind in Mexico.

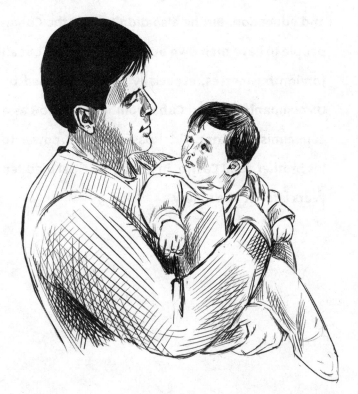

CHAPTER 8
The Cuban Revolution

Besides Che, Fidel had recruited about eighty other men in Mexico to join his army. Che and the others went to an abandoned farm about twenty miles outside Mexico City for training. Che knew the army they would face in Cuba was much bigger, and it had a lot more weapons than they had. Their small rebel army couldn't win if they tried to go up against them directly. Instead, they had to fight in a style called guerrilla warfare.

Guerrilla Warfare

The word *guerrilla* means "little war" in Spanish. Guerrilla warfare sometimes takes place when a small group of fighters take on a much bigger and more skilled army. The smaller group knows that they can't win by fighting their bigger and stronger opponent with a traditional attack. Instead, they have to sneak up on their enemy and surprise them. Once they do this, they quickly retreat back into hiding, then attack again at another spot at a different time. They are fighting "little wars." In between attacks, the smaller group, the guerrillas, tries to hide as best they can—usually in forests or dense jungles.

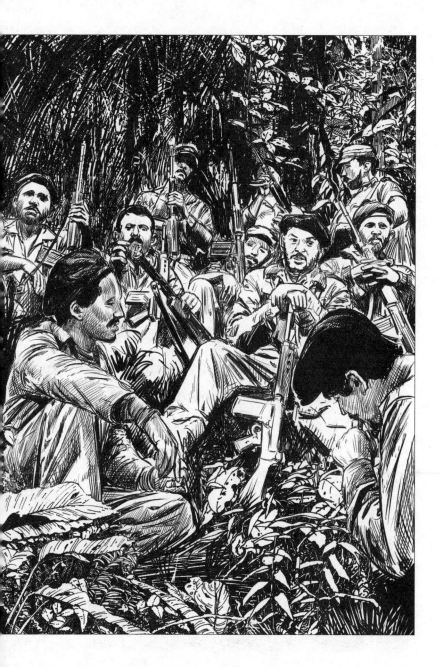

Even though Che was joining the group as a doctor, he learned to fight, too. In training, Che was taught how to use weapons, how to sneak up on enemies, and how to survive on mountains and in forests. Despite his asthma, Che excelled at the training. In some ways, it wasn't much different from the wild play he had done as a young boy. His instructor called him "the best guerrilla of them all."

The attack on Cuba—an island nation just ninety miles off the coast of Florida—was planned for November 1956. Che said goodbye to his wife and new daughter, then boarded a boat named *Granma*. The sixty-foot boat was built to hold

only twelve people, but they crammed eighty-two men aboard. It took them over a week to make the nearly 1,200-mile trip from Mexico to Cuba. The crossing was rough—food was limited, and many of the men became seasick.

Once they arrived, the men on the *Granma* discovered Cuba's south coast was well guarded.

As they made their way ashore, they were showered by gunfire from dictator Batista's army. The men scattered into a sugarcane field to escape the flying bullets. Che was shot in the neck, but the wound was not serious. The survivors scrambled into the mountains. Only twelve men, including Che and Fidel, were still alive. At one point during the escape, Che made an important decision:

"I had before me
a pack filled with
medicines and a
case of ammunition.
The two were too
heavy to be carried
together," explained
Che. "I took the
case of ammunition,
leaving behind the
medicine."

Right there and
then, Che decided
he wasn't just a
doctor anymore. He
was a fighter.

CHAPTER 9
Attack, Retreat, Repeat

Fidel, Che, and their tiny rebel group fought the Cuban army over the next two years. The rebels hid in the mountains. They would sometimes walk for days, collapsing only when it became too dark to continue. Some days Che had so much trouble breathing, he used his rifle as a walking stick. Still he kept going.

The rebel army met many peasants who lived

in the mountains. Che gained their trust by treating the sick people among them. Many of the farmers had never even seen a doctor in their entire lives. As Che helped them, he described the rebels' cause. Che said that once they overthrew the current government, life in Cuba would become much better.

The peasants soon began helping the rebels. They gave them food, water, and even let them sleep in their homes. Che and Fidel asked the Cuban people they met in the mountains to join them in their fight to overthrow Batista. Many said yes. The rebel army, which began with just twelve men, grew bigger and bigger. In between their sneak attacks, Che taught some of the peasants to read and write. By teaching them, he was also gaining their trust and support.

"A country that does not know how to read and write is easy to deceive," Che explained.

Che was a brave fighter who was willing to battle on the front lines. He never asked any of his soldiers to do anything he wouldn't do himself. The troops attacked different army posts across Cuba. After they attacked, the rebels retreated back into the mountains and hid until it was safe to strike again. Their life was a constant cycle of attack, retreat, and repeat. Fidel soon promoted Che to second in charge and gave him the new title of *comandante*, or commander. Che said he was "the proudest man in the world that day."

In between battles, Che read or wrote in his journal, sitting up late into the night while smoking a cigar or pipe. Smoking was an especially bad habit for Che, who already had trouble breathing. But the mosquitoes were always on attack in the hot and humid jungle. The smoke helped keep them away.

The rebel army set up a radio station at one of their posts in the mountains. Che and Fidel were able to use it to promote their cause to Cuban citizens to gain their support. The revolution was big news around the world, especially in the United States. Reporters from newspapers like the *New York Times* trekked into the mountains of Cuba. They took photographs and interviewed Fidel, Che, and other guerrilla fighters. Che spoke in a low and calm voice, telling them how they were trying to improve the lives of the poor. Reporters wrote what Che said and described him as having kind eyes and a warm smile. Reading these stories, many people began to see Che as a hero.

On January 1, 1959, a little over two years since the fighting began, Che and his troops took over the city of Santa Clara. The city in the middle of Cuba was the heart of the country's railway and highway system. This rebel army, which had started out as just a small band of men, had taken over one of the most important cities in Cuba. It was nothing short of a miracle. When Batista

found out that Santa Clara had been captured, he resigned as president and fled to the Dominican Republic, a neighboring island.

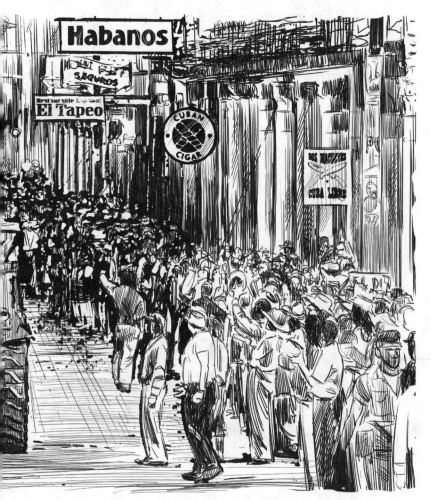

On January 2, Che and his troops left Santa Clara to begin their march into Havana, the capital of Cuba. People lined the streets and chanted *"Viva la revolución,"* which means "Long live the revolution" in Spanish. Fidel, Che, and the rebel army had won the war. Che was only thirty years old. Cuba was their country to lead.

The Cuban Revolution Map

This is the path that Che, Fidel, and their rebel army took in Cuba to achieve victory and eventually march into the capital city of Havana. The men traveled on foot, or sometimes on horseback, fighting many small battles the entire way.

Che felt that the victory in Cuba would be an inspiration for the rest of Latin America—basically, all of Central and South America where Spanish, French, and Portuguese are spoken. "This revolution should set an example for all  of Latin America," he said. But even as Che spoke, he knew he would only help lead Cuba for a short time. He had bigger ideas. Che wanted to bring the spirit of revolution to countries all over the world.

CHAPTER 10
A Cuban Leader

Once Che and Fidel took over Cuba, they became celebrities around the world. Reporters loved to interview them and take their pictures. In many of the photographs, Che looks like a cool teenager. He has a sly smile, twinkling eyes, and a messy but appealing style.

"We have demonstrated that a small group of men who are determined, supported by their people, and without fear of dying, can overcome a disciplined regular army and defeat it," Che said.

Che's wife and daughter traveled to Cuba. Che and Hilda had not seen each other in over two years, but it wasn't a happy reunion. Che told Hilda that he had fallen in love with a young Cuban woman who had joined the rebel army. Hilda and Che soon divorced, and Che married Aleida March on June 2, 1959.

Fidel named Che an "official" Cuban citizen once the war ended and told him they would lead their country together. One of the first laws Che wrote was called the "Agrarian Reform Law." It was similar to what President Árbenz of Guatemala had done when Che was living there. Under this law, any one person could own one thousand acres of land. Any more than that would have to be given to the government, which would redistribute it.

Che also banned foreigners from owning land in Cuba, especially sugarcane fields, which made a lot of money for outside businesses. Che always wanted to get those "gringos" out of Latin America. Here was finally his chance to do so.

Under Fidel and Che, free health care and education were offered to every citizen of Cuba. Illiteracy—not knowing how to read or write—became a thing of the past. For all the good he did, Che also ran a prison in Havana where those who were against Castro's communist ideas were jailed. Some prisoners were tortured and even killed there.

Che was also put in charge of the National Bank of Cuba. It was a funny position for a man who didn't care very much about money. Since taking over Cuba, Che had refused to be paid a salary. He lived in a small house and dressed simply in his military uniform. When he wasn't governing, he volunteered in the fields on Sundays, cutting down sugarcane. Che wanted to run Cuba's economy so that everybody—including himself—had the same amount of money and land.

The United States had businesses
that owned a lot of land in Cuba
for growing sugarcane. They
didn't want to be forced to
leave. Because of the Cold
War, the United States
was afraid of having an
unfriendly communist
country so close to
its borders.

Sugarcane

Because it feared that the new communist
government would force US businesses out, the
United States invaded Cuba on April 17, 1961.
Over one thousand soldiers invaded the southeast
coast of Cuba at the Bay of Pigs. They were mostly
Cubans who had been living in Florida and
trained by US forces. Fidel and Che were ready
for them. They pulled together over two hundred
thousand men to fight the assault. Within hours,
the fight was easily won by Che and the Cubans.

The Cold War (1945–1991)

After World War II ended in 1945, the United States and the Soviet Union, a communist nation, were the two most influential countries in the world. These superpowers never actually fought each other with weapons on the battlefield. Instead, they engaged in a battle of ideas—a "cold" war. The two sides were defending democratic forms of government and communism. During the Cold War, the United States believed it had to defend democracy against the spread of communism in countries like Korea, Germany, Vietnam, and Cuba. The Cold War ended in 1991 when the Soviet Union collapsed.

The Bay of Pigs was a huge victory for Cuba—and a giant embarrassment for the United States. It made Fidel and Che even more popular with many of the Cuban people. Later, Che even famously thanked the United States for the victory.

The Bay of Pigs success was short-lived. Fidel and Che—and the whole world—soon had bigger problems to deal with.

Because Cuba was a communist country, the Soviet Union, the most powerful communist

country in the world at the time, sent money to support them. And in 1962, the Soviet Union decided to send nuclear missiles to Cuba as well. If any of those missiles were launched, the entire eastern United States could be destroyed.

When the United States learned about the Soviet missiles, they demanded that they be removed from Cuba. At first, the Soviet Union refused. But after two tense weeks, during which the entire world worried about a nuclear war, the two superpowers made a deal: The missiles were removed, and in return, the United States promised not to attack Cuba. The US and Soviet leaders reached their agreement without consulting Fidel and Che. This made the two men furious. If it had been up to them, they would have kept the nuclear missiles in Cuba.

CHAPTER 11
A Revolutionary Once More

In December 1964, Che, now thirty-six years old, traveled to the United Nations headquarters in New York City. He represented Cuba as its minister of industry.

The United Nations

The United Nations (UN) was founded in October 1945, right after the end of World War II, with the hope of preventing more world wars. The UN has more than 190 members, who have equal representation in the General Assembly. The main goal of the member nations is to maintain world peace. The United Nations also tries to protect human rights. They fight disease and famine, and they help refugees all over the world.

Che spoke to the General Assembly of the UN. He criticized the United States and other countries for taking advantage of the land and the people of poorer nations. He said the United States was like an "animal feeding on the helpless."

It didn't make sense for large US businesses to own the land and make money in places where the people were so very poor. They were the very laborers who were making foreign businesses rich. Che saw the United States as a big bully who pushed weaker countries around.

While Che was speaking at the United Nations, many protesters on the streets chanted angry insults. Che remained calm. He believed in what he said. Che didn't care if other people didn't agree with him. He was willing to die for his beliefs. He ended his speech by saying, *"Patria o muerte!"*— homeland or death.

When Che left New York, he went on a three-month tour around the world. He continued to give speeches about big countries, especially the United States, taking advantage of small countries.

Che returned home to Cuba on March 15, 1965. Reporters and photographers rushed to greet him as he got off the plane. They took

some of the last photos ever seen of Che.

Che disappeared from Cuba less than a month after his arrival. He left behind his wife, Aleida, their four small children, and his oldest daughter,

Hildita. It wasn't easy. But Che had done it when he came to Cuba years ago, and he was able to do it again. Che believed he had to sacrifice the love of his family for the love of *all* people. He left to start another revolution.

"The true revolutionary is guided by a great feeling of love," Che wrote. "We must strive every day so that this love of living humanity will be transformed into actual deeds.

"The leaders of the revolution have children who do not learn to call their father with their first word." Che also wrote that "they have wives who must be part of the general sacrifice. Their friends are strictly limited to their comrades in revolution. There is no life outside of the revolution."

Everyone, including Fidel and Aleida, claimed they didn't know where Che was. Months went by. Newspapers and television programs around the world wondered, Where is Che? Finally, in October 1965, Fidel appeared on television and read a farewell letter he had received from his friend.

In the letter, Che said goodbye to Cuba. He explained that he left to start revolutions in other parts of the world, just as he had planned to years ago. He never intended to stay in Cuba forever, and now he was fulfilling a promise he had made to himself. Che didn't see starting a revolution as a choice. He was determined to help the poor of the world—even if he had to use violence to do it. He wrote, "On new battlefields I will carry with me . . . the revolutionary spirit of my people . . . to fight . . . wherever it may be."

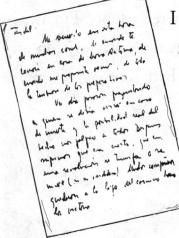

He signed the letter in part "To victory forever."

CHAPTER 12
Where in the World Is . . . Che?

When Che left Cuba in late March 1965, he was already famous. If he was going to help other countries, he had to do it secretly. He cut his hair, shaved his beard, and put on a regular suit and tie to look like a businessman. He traveled without being recognized.

Che first went to the Congo, a country in Africa led by a terrible dictator. Che wanted to organize a guerrilla army to overthrow their leader just like he had done in Cuba. But once in the Congo, Che's army was unable to overcome many difficulties. Che also became very sick in the African jungle. He lost close to forty pounds. Less than a year in, Che abandoned his revolutionary fight in the Congo. He sneaked back into Cuba and stayed quiet for a couple of months. Then he traveled in disguise to Bolivia, in South America, to try to overthrow the dictator there.

When Che arrived in Bolivia in November 1966, he had trouble organizing enough men to fight. He was also short on supplies and weapons. Che had set up his army's home base in a rain forest on the banks of the Amazon River. The conditions were even rougher than they had been during the Cuban Revolution. Che's men battled raging water, steep terrain, and vines with vicious thorns. The rain forest air made Che's asthma worse, and he ran out of medicine to keep it under control. Without asthma medicine, he could barely walk. He rode a mule instead, coughing the entire time.

Unlike the Cuban Revolution—when Che was able to convince peasants to join his cause—he couldn't seem to rally Bolivian citizens. Many of the poor farmers thought Che and his small army were drug dealers. They didn't understand their cause. And they didn't trust them.

"The guerrilla is supported by the peasant and worker masses," Che wrote in one of his journals. "Without them, guerrilla warfare is not possible."

The Bolivian government soon learned that Che had sneaked into their country to start a revolution. Government officials offered reward money to anybody who could tell them where Che was. A local farmer soon reported the location of Che's camp. The Bolivian army captured Che on October 8, 1967, less than a year after he'd arrived in the country.

One day later, Che was killed by a firing squad—a group of soldiers given the task of shooting someone. He was thirty-nine years old. It was reported that his last words were, "I know you are here to kill me. Shoot, coward, you are only killing a man."

With these words, Che meant that by getting rid of one person, you cannot stop a revolution. He knew his revolutionary spirit would live on. Che Guevara was buried in a small village in Bolivia. The Bolivian government wanted it this way. They didn't want people to visit Che's grave as if he had been a hero.

Fidel Castro told the world the news about Che's death. He gave a tribute speech about Che in a plaza in Havana and almost a million people came to listen.

"Che died defending no other cause than the cause of the poor and the humble of this earth," Fidel said. "And the selflessness with which he defended that cause cannot be disputed even by his most bitter enemies.

"If we wish to express what we want our children to be," Fidel continued, "we must say from our very hearts . . . we want them to be like Che!"

Che's Grave

After Che Guevara was killed, his body was buried in an unmarked grave in Bolivia for thirty years. Finally, Cuban officials learned where he was buried, dug up his remains, and brought them back to Cuba. Che's body was then buried in Santa Clara, Cuba, on October 18, 1997.

Today at his gravesite there is a statue of Che, a museum about his life, and an eternal flame lit by Fidel Castro in honor of his partner in the revolution.

Chapter 13
The Man, the Myth, the Legend

To this day, people still wave posters of Che, wear Che T-shirts, and even put on Che berets while marching for civil rights or protesting against unjust wars. His fighting spirit has become even more important to people around the world since his death.

Che's image can be found on T-shirts, hats, posters, album covers, wine bottles, and even sunglasses. One photograph of Che wearing a beret, his olive green uniform, a tense stare, and a scruffy beard is one of the most reproduced images of all time.

Around the world, people remember Che as a friend to the poor and an enemy of the rich and greedy. And some remember him as Castro's violent political ally. He tried to help people who didn't know how to stand up for themselves. "If you tremble with indignation at every injustice, then you are a comrade of mine," Che said.

In recent years, many movies have been made about Che's life, including *The Motorcycle Diaries* in 2004, and *Che* in 2008.

Before Che died, he had written a letter to his five children so they could better understand how their father lived and what he died for. Che wrote:

"Your father has been a man who acted according to his beliefs. . . . Above all, try always to be able to feel deeply any injustice committed against any person in any part of the world. It is the most beautiful quality of a revolutionary."

Che lived his life exactly how he wanted and never compromised.

The Famous Photograph

In 1960, photographer Alberto Korda was at a funeral in Cuba working for a local newspaper. He was taking photographs of Fidel Castro. But Alberto also took pictures of the people around Fidel, including Che Guevara.

Che stood stiffly wearing his uniform, a rough beard, and his hair long underneath a beret. Alberto said he was drawn to the power and confidence of Che's face, which also showed "anger and pain." The paper didn't use that photo, but years after Che died, the photograph was finally printed. This image of Che—among the most popular portraits in the world—came to represent the very act of protest itself. It is one of the most famous photographs of the twentieth century.

El Che Vive! This means Che, and his ideals, will live on forever.

(Ever onward to victory!)

Che On Screen

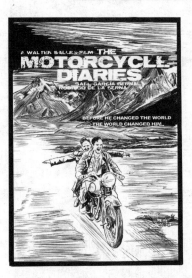

The Motorcycle Diaries is based on Che's adventures with his friend Alberto Granado as they travel through South America as young men. Alberto said, "The film shows what we were, which was two young men—boys, really—who went looking for adventure and found the truth and tragedy of our homeland."

"We were reenacting a journey that was done fifty years ago," said Gael García Bernal, who plays Che in *The Motorcycle Diaries*. "And what is surprising is that the social problems of Latin America are the same today. Which is heartbreaking in a way, but it also makes you feel how important it is to tell the story."

Che, starring Benicio del Toro, is about Che's time as a revolutionary in Cuba and other countries.

Timeline of Che Guevara's Life

1928	Ernesto "Che" Guevara is born on June 14, 1928, in Rosario, Argentina
1948	Enrolls in medical school
1951	Sets out on a five-thousand-mile journey around South America with his friend Alberto Granado, and keeps a journal of the entire trip
1953	Graduates from medical school and sets off on a second journey through South and Central America
1955	Marries Hilda Gadea on August 18
1956	Daughter, Hildita, is born on February 15
	Sails to Cuba to begin the Cuban revolution
1959	With Fidel Castro, declares victory in the Cuban Revolution
	Divorces Hilda Gadea
	Marries Aleida March
1964	Speaks at the UN General Assembly in New York
1965	Secretly travels to the Congo in Africa
1966	Travels to Bolivia in South America
1967	Is executed on October 9 in Bolivia
1993	Che's journal entries from his 1952 trip are published as a book, *The Motorcycle Diaries*
1997	Che's remains are brought from Bolivia to Cuba
2017	The fiftieth anniversary of Che's death is remembered

Timeline of the World

1928 — The first Winter Olympics are held in St. Moritz, Switzerland, February 11–19

1932 — Amelia Earhart is the first woman to fly solo nonstop across the Atlantic Ocean

1939 — World War II begins

1945 — World War II ends

1950 — The Korean War begins

1953 — Ernest Hemingway wins a Pulitzer Prize for *The Old Man and the Sea*

1958 — Bobby Fisher, age fourteen, wins the United States Chess Championship

1961 — John F. Kennedy is sworn in as the thirty-fifth president of the United States on January 20

1962 — The first-ever Walmart store opens on July 2 in Rogers, Arkansas

1963 — Martin Luther King Jr. reads his "I Have a Dream" speech on August 28 in Washington, DC

1964 — United States Surgeon General reports for the first time that smoking is bad for your health

1966 — The Black Panther Party for Self-Defense, an African American revolutionary party known simply as the Black Panthers, is formed in Oakland, California

1969 — Neil Armstrong is the first person to walk on the moon

Bibliography

*Books for young readers

Anderson, John Lee. *Che*. New York: Grove Press, 1997.

Guevara, Ernesto Che. *Congo Diary*. Melbourne, Australia: Ocean Press, 2011.

Guevara, Ernesto Che. *Latin America Diaries*. Melbourne, Australia: Ocean Press, 2011.

Guevara, Ernesto Che. *The Motorcycle Diaries*. Melbourne, Australia: Ocean Press, 2003.

Guevara, Ernesto Che. *Reminiscences of the Cuban Revolutionary War*. Melbourne, Australia: Ocean Press, 2006.

James, Daniel. *Che Guevara: A Biography*. New York: First Cooper Square Press Edition, 2001.

*Shimano, Chie, and Kiyoshi Konno. *Che Guevara: A Manga Biography*. New York: Penguin Books, 2008.

Sinclair, Andrew. *Che Guevara*. New York: Viking Press, 1970.